# Flowering Plants

Written by
**Beth Davis**

Cover Design by
Matthew Van Zomeren

Inside Art by
Roberta Collier Morales

Publishers
Instructional Fair • TS Denison
Grand Rapids, Michigan 49544

## About the Book

The Inquiry Science series was designed and tested by classroom teachers familiar with the National Science Education Standards. It is the goal of the series to apply the standards in a user-friendly format.

Promote minds-on learning by challenging the students to verbalize their observations and make inferences. Ask simple questions such as the following: What just happened? Why do you think that happened? What did you discover? Where have you seen that before? The science process skills used in each lesson are provided so you can raise students' awareness and highlight their importance.

## Credits

Author: Beth Davis
Cover Design: Matthew Van Zomeren
Inside Illustrations: Roberta Collier Morales
Project Director/Editor: Elizabeth Flikkema
Editors: Wendy Roh Jenks, Linda Triemstra
Page Design: Pat Geasler

## About the Author

Beth Davis is an outstanding educator from Miami, Florida, where she is currently a science lab teacher for grades 2–5. Ms. Davis received her Bachelor of Science in Elementary Education from Florida International University. Her master's degree was earned at Nova University. Beth Davis has written curriculum and several articles in the areas of math and science. Her other Instructional Fair • TS Denison book is titled *Matter* and is also found in the Inquiry Science series.

Standard Book Number: 1-56822-678-0
*Flowering Plants*—Grades 2–3
Copyright © 1999 by Ideal • Instructional Fair Publishing Group
a division of Tribune Education
2400 Turner Avenue NW
Grand Rapids, Michigan 49544

# Table of Contents

## Seed Sort

Exploring the attributes of seeds ................ 4–5

## Fruity Tooty

Students will cut open fruits and
observe the seeds ......................................... 6–7

## Do Plants Need Light?

Students will conduct an experiment
to determine whether plants can grow
in a dark place .............................................. 8–9

## Do Plants Need Water?

Students will conduct an experiment
to determine whether plants can grow
without water ........................................... 10–11

## Soil Soak

Exploring the properties of soils .............. 12–13

## Super Stem!

Discovering the function of the stem ....... 14–15

## Found a Peanut

Measuring and observing a peanut ......... 16–17

## Seed Sprouts

Observing and sprouting seeds ............... 18–19

## Herbicides and Pesticides

Students play a food-chain game ............ 20–21

## Onion-Skin Cells

Observing cells under a microscope ........ 22–23

## Dissecting a Flower

Students observe the parts of a
real flower .............................................. 24–25

## Life Cycle of a Flowering Plant

Students draw the stages of the
life cycle of a plant .................................. 26–27

## Investigating a Pumpkin

Exploring the attributes of pumpkins ...... 28–29

## Erosion and Plants

Exploring the factors that
reduce erosion ......................................... 30–31

## Performance-Based Assessment

A rubric of student performance ................... 32

# Seed Sort

## Gearing Up

Hold a discussion about individual differences. Brainstorm a list of attributes such as blue eyes, curly hair, and wearing blue pants. Secretly choose two attributes and sort several students according to those attributes. Ask the class why the students were sorted the way that they were. Sort again by different attributes such as size, type of clothing, or shoe type. Once students have an understanding about sorting and classifying, explain that seeds can also be sorted by attributes.

*Process Skills Used*

- classifying
- graphing
- observing
- recording data

## Guided Discovery

**Background information for the teacher:**
Seeds come in different sizes and shapes and are surrounded by fruit. Different types of fruit have a different number of seeds inside of them.

**Materials needed for each group:**
small cup of a variety of the following seeds or beans, such as corn (popcorn), lima beans, kidney beans, green peas, and sunflower seeds.

**Directions for the activity:**
Distribute the mixed seeds and beans to each group. Before beginning, have students predict how many of each type of seeds there are. Instruct students to sort the seeds, count how many there are of each, record the number on the data table, and graph the results.

## Responding to Discovery

Talk about other ways to sort the seeds such as color, size, and shape.

## Applications and Extensions

Compile the data on a class graph. Discuss the data.

*Real-World Applications*

- Ask students to bring in seeds from different foods.

IF20849 *Flowering Plants*

Name _____

# Seed Sort

## Data Table

| Name the seed. | Draw the seed. | Predict the number of seeds. | Count the seeds. |
|---|---|---|---|
| 1. | | | |
| 2. | | | |
| 3. | | | |
| 4. | | | |
| 5. | | | |

Sort seeds here:

| 1 | 2 | 3 | 4 | 5 |
|---|---|---|---|---|
| | | | | |

Graph the number of seeds you found of each kind.

### Seed graph

| Number of seeds | | | | | |
|---|---|---|---|---|---|
| 20 | | | | | |
| 18 | | | | | |
| 16 | | | | | |
| 14 | | | | | |
| 12 | | | | | |
| 10 | | | | | |
| 8 | | | | | |
| 6 | | | | | |
| 4 | | | | | |
| 2 | | | | | |

_____ _____ _____ _____ _____

### Types of seeds

IF20849 *Flowering Plants*

# Fruity Tooty

## Gearing Up

Ask students to think about the last time they ate a piece of fruit. Did they cut it up and remove the seeds? How many seeds were in the fruit? Ask students to name fruits they like and how many seeds might be in each one.

*Process Skills Used*
- predicting
- graphing
- observing
- recording data
- comparing

## Guided Discovery

**Background information for the teacher:**
All flowering plants come from seeds. Seeds grow inside and are protected by the fruit of the plant. Seeds contain the food that is needed for a plant to sprout.

**Materials needed for each group:**
A variety of fruits (choose fruits with a variety of numbers of seeds inside.)
paper plates
paper towels

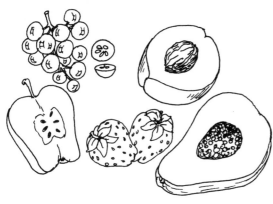

## Directions for the activity:

You can use any type of fruit. Some suggestions: apple, peach, pear, cantaloupe or other melon, and pomegranate. Before cutting open the fruits, have students predict which fruit will contain the most and the fewest seeds. Next, instruct students to remove the seeds and count the seeds in each. Record the number of seeds on the data table.

## Responding to Discovery

Which fruit had the most seeds? Which had the fewest? Did the size of the fruit determine how many seeds it had?

## Applications and Extensions

Plant the seeds. Label the pots. Keep a record of care and growth.

*Real-World Applications*
- Think about the foods you eat. List foods that come from seeds.

Name _____

# Fruity Tooty

| Name the fruit. | Predict how many seeds. | Record the actual number of seeds. |
|---|---|---|
| | | |
| | | |
| | | |
| | | |
| | | |

Draw each fruit and one of its seeds.

| | | | | |
|---|---|---|---|---|
| Seed: | Seed: | Seed: | Seed: | Seed: |

- Which fruit had the largest number of seeds? _____

- Which fruit had the smallest number of seeds? _____

IF20849 *Flowering Plants*

# Do Plants Need Light?

## Gearing Up

Ask the class, "Could we live on Earth without the sun?" Hold a class discussion about the importance of the sun. List all the jobs of the sun. Tell students that today's discovery explores one of the jobs of the sun.

*Process Skills Used*
- predicting
- observing
- recording data

## Guided Discovery

**Background information for the teacher:**
Just as plants need water in order to grow, they also need light. Light is crucial for plants to create their own food. Plants use the energy from the sun to undergo photosynthesis. During the process of photosynthesis, carbon dioxide is changed to carbohydrates and oxygen. In this activity, students will see what an important role light plays in plant growth.

**Materials needed for each small group:**
2 clear plastic cups
soil
seeds (soaked sunflower seeds grow quickly)
water
one small box

**Directions for the activity:**
Have students fill both cups ¾ full with soil. Plant two to four seeds on the edges of the soil so students can observe the roots of the plant as they grow. Place one plant in a sunny location and place the other in the classroom under a box so that it gets no light. Students fill in their data tables each day while the plants are growing. When the first leaves on the plant in the light can be seen, remove the plant from the box and observe the differences. The experiment may take longer than a week. If so, duplicate the chart and continue marking the data.

## Responding to Discovery

Have students draw conclusions about why the plant in the box did not grow. Ask students if they think plants could have too much sunlight. Discuss a way you could prove that hypothesis.

## Applications and Extensions

Place a brick on a patch of grass. Remove it a week later to discover what happens to the grass that does not receive any sunlight.

*Real-World Applications*
- Discuss the number of daylight hours and the amount of daylight in Alaska.

IF20849 *Flowering Plants*

# Do Plants Need Light?

🌱 Plants need food, water, and sunlight to grow. Will a seed sprout, grow, and produce leaves in the dark?

Make a prediction. _____

_____

🌱 Plant seeds in two cups. Place one in the light and one in the dark.

🌱 Treat both cups exactly alike except for the amount of light. Keep track of what you do and observe for a week.

| Plant 1 Location | Amount of water | Observations (color, height, width, shape) |
|---|---|---|
| Day 1 | | |
| Day 2 | | |
| Day 3 | | |
| Day 4 | | |
| Day 5 | | |
| Day 6 | | |
| Day 7 | | |
| Plant 2 Location | Amount of water | Observations |
| Day 1 | | |
| Day 2 | | |
| Day 3 | | |
| Day 4 | | |
| Day 5 | | |
| Day 6 | | |
| Day 7 | | |

# Do Plants Need Water?

## Gearing Up

Ask the class, "Could we live on Earth without water?" Hold a class discussion about the importance of water. List all the uses of water. Tell students that today's discovery explores one use of water.

> ### *Process Skills Used*
> - observing
> - recording data
> - making predictions

## Guided Discovery

**Background information for the teacher:**
All living things need water in order to grow. At the seed stage, water is important to soften the seed coat. As the plant grows, water carries important nutrients through the soil to the plant. Plants get water naturally through precipitation. In this activity, students will test whether a plant can live without water.

**Materials needed for each small group:**
two small containers
(cups or milk cartons)
lima beans
soil

**Directions for the activity:**
Have students partially fill each container with soil. Soak one seed (you may prepare this in advance) and place it in the soil. Place the other seed in the soil without any water. Be sure to label one container "wet" and the other "dry." The group should lightly water (as needed) the plant labeled "wet." Each day, the students record observations on their data.

## Responding to Discovery

Discuss the results of the experiment. What is the role of water? Ask students to write a paragraph explaining the importance of water to Earth.

## Applications and Extensions

Place radish seeds on a wet sponge. Keep the sponge moist. Observe the seeds over several days. Draw the results.

> ### *Real-World Applications*
> - Discuss the implications of drought on plants and humans.

# Do Plants Need Water?

🐛 List some of the uses of water.

_____

_____

🐛 Do you think that a plant can grow without water? _____

After you have planted your beans, record each day
what you do and observe.

|  | **Bean with water** | **Bean without water** |
|---|---|---|
| Day 1 | Plant the bean and add water. | Plant the bean. |
| Day 2 | | |
| Day 3 | | |
| Day 4 | | |
| Day 5 | | |
| Day 6 | | |
| Day 7 | | |
| Day 8 | | |
| Day 9 | | |
| Day 10 | | |

🐛 Which plant grew better, the
plant with water or the plant
without? Draw and label each
plant.

IF20849 *Flowering Plants*

# Soil Soak

## Gearing Up

Ask students the following questions: Have you ever seen fruits or vegetables growing in a field? Where was the field located? Have you ever seen fruits or vegetables growing on the beach? Why do you think you haven't? Tell students that in this discovery, we will explore the differences between soil and sand.

### Process Skills Used
- classifying
- inferring
- observing
- recording data
- measuring

## Guided Discovery

**Background information for the teacher:**
Rich soil contains a combination of organic matter and ground rock (sand). Soil absorbs, or holds, water. If the soil can hold the water the roots of the plants have time to absorb and use the water. Water flows through sand quickly, not allowing the roots of plants time to absorb the water. Soils that allow water to percolate through are said to be more permeable than are those that absorb water.

**Materials needed for each small group:**
4 plastic cups
beakers for measuring
200 mL of potting soil
200 mL sand
300 mL water
a safety pin

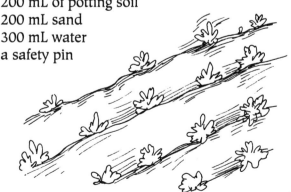

## Directions for the activity:

Gently poke eight small holes in the bottom of each cup with the safety pin. Place sand in one cup and dirt in the other. Hold the filled cups over the other two empty cups so the empty cups can catch the water. Pour 150 ml of water over each cup of soil at the same time. Observe the water for 2–5 minutes. Measure the amount of water in the bottom cups. Compare. Record your observations on the activity sheet.

## Responding to Discovery

Which earth material would be better for planting? Why do you think so?

## Applications and Extensions

Plant seeds in soil and in sand. Be sure they both are exposed to light and are watered regularly. See for yourself which one is best for plant growth.

### Real-World Applications
- Fruits and vegetables are best planted in soil that is rich in nutrients. The soil allows the water to reach the root of the plants. You would never see these types of plants planted at the beach!

Name _____

# Soil Soak

sand / soil

🌻 Measure 200 mL of sand and potting soil into the cups. Pour 150 mL of water into each soil. Watch the water drain into the second set of cups.

🌻 Measure the water collected.

     sand _____ mL       potting soil _____ mL

🌻 Make a bar graph of the amount of water absorbed by each soil. (Subtract the collected water from the beginning amount.)

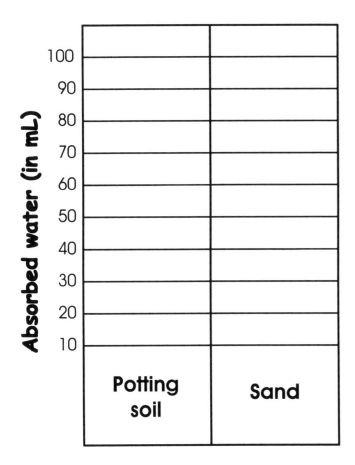

sand _____ mL

potting soil _____ mL

🌻 Which soil absorbs the most water?

_____

🌻 Why is the potting soil a better choice for growing plants?

_____

_____

_____

_____

IF20849 *Flowering Plants*

# Super Stem!

## Gearing Up

Ask your students, "What do you think stems are good for?" Some ideas may include . . . stems hold up flowers, they can be edible (celery), they give strength to a plant, or they bring water up from the roots.

*Process Skills Used*
- observing
- comparing
- predicting
- recording data

## Guided Discovery

**Background information for the teacher:**
Stems have many important functions in the growth of a plant. One thing a stem does is act as a support system holding the plant upright so that it can reach toward the sun. Another important function the stem has is to act as a transport system. Water and minerals are carried through the stem to the roots and leaves of the plant. Students can observe the movement of liquids through the stem in this activity.

**Materials needed for each small group:**
a 6 oz. (180 ml) plastic cup
water
blue or red food coloring
white carnation

## Directions for the activity:

Cut off the bottom of the carnation stem. Pour about 3 oz. (90ml) of water into the cup. Add 8 drops of food coloring. Place the cut flower in the cup. Leave the flower overnight and observe what happens.

## Responding to Discovery

Discuss:
- Why did the carnation turn from white to colored?
- What is one job of a stem, and why are stems important?

## Applications and Extensions

Repeat the same activity using celery stalks.

*Real-World Applications*
- Soil nutrients
- Coloring/dying flowers
- Veins as transport systems

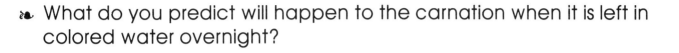

Name _____

# Super Stem!

❧ What do you predict will happen to the carnation when it is left in colored water overnight?

_____

_____

| Color the carnation as it looked before it was left in the colored water. | Color what happened to the carnation that was left in the colored water overnight. |
|---|---|
|  |  |

❧ What happened when the carnation was left in the colored water overnight?

_____

_____

❧ Why did it happen?

_____

_____

❧ What is the job of a stem, and why is the stem important to the plant?

_____

_____

IF20849 *Flowering Plants*

# Found a Peanut

## Gearing Up

Put a spoonful of peanut butter in a baby food jar. Ask the students to use their senses of smell and sight to observe the substance. Can they guess what it is? **Caution:** Before performing this experiment, find out if any students are allergic to peanuts. For the sake of those children, do not conduct the experiment.

*Process Skills Used*
- observing
- predicting
- estimating
- measuring

## Guided Discovery

**Background information for the teacher:** Peanuts are legumes. A legume is a fruit that comes in a pod or shell that often contains more than one seed. Many products can be made from peanuts. Peanut butter is a very popular way to eat peanuts. Peanuts are an excellent source of protein. The peanut consists of almost 50% oil. The peanut shell also has uses. The shells are ground into a powder which is used to make plastics, cork substitutes, and some abrasives.

**Materials needed for each group:**
a bowl of peanuts in the shell
string
a scale
a centimeter ruler

**Directions for the activity:**
Each student selects one peanut from the bowl that he or she will get to know through observation. Have students record on their papers drawings and written observations about their peanuts. Students may use the string to measure the length and circumference. After recording the information on their worksheets, students return the peanuts to the bowls and mix the peanuts. Challenge students to find their original peanuts. Then, direct students to exchange their notes with teammates and try to identify the described peanuts.

## Responding to Discovery

Ask students to describe the most useful observations in finding the original peanut.

## Applications and Extensions

Put shelled peanuts in the blender and make peanut butter. Add oil and salt, if desired. Serve on crackers.

*Real-World Applications*
- Have students research and list several products that are made from peanuts.

# Found a Peanut

☙ Draw your peanut from 2 or 3 views.

☙ List as many observations as you can about your peanut. Be sure to include color, texture, size, mass, and other features that will help you to identify it once it has been returned to the bowl.

_____

_____

_____

_____

_____

_____

☙ Use your string to measure from end to end on your peanut. How many centimeters long is it? _____

☙ Wrap the string around the peanut. What is the circumference? _____

☙ What is your peanut's mass in grams? _____

☙ List all of the uses you can think of for a peanut.

_____

_____

_____

_____

_____

IF20849 *Flowering Plants*

# Seed Sprouts

## Gearing Up

Soak overnight enough lima bean seeds for every one or two students in your class. Provide magnifying glasses so students can find and identify the seed coat, cotyledon (nutritious part), and the tiny sprout known as the plumule. Ask the students to predict how long they think it takes for a seed to sprout.

*Process Skills Used*
- predicting
- observing
- recording data

## Guided Discovery

**Background information for the teacher:**
The sprouting of a seed is known as germination. Before germination, the seed absorbs water and swells. The swelling splits the seed coat so the seedling can emerge. Some seeds germinate much faster than others. In this activity, students will plant several types of seeds on a sponge and observe which type germinates the fastest.

**Materials needed for each small group:**
One well-soaked sponge
container of water
one plate to set the sponge on (a Styrofoam tray works well and encourages recycling)
mustard seeds
radish seeds
grass seeds
lima bean seeds

**Directions for the activity:**
Students place the sponge in a container of water until it has soaked up all of the water that it can hold. Place it on the tray or plate. Visually divide the sponge into four sections and cover each section with a different type of seed. Check the sponge garden on a daily basis as some of the seeds will begin to sprout very quickly. Water may be added, as needed. Record observations on page 19.

## Responding to Discovery

Which type of seed began to germinate first? Describe the roots that you saw for each type of seed. Were there any similarities or differences?

## Applications and Extensions

Form a hypothesis about what types of seeds germinate quickly. Gather more evidence to confirm your hypothesis.

*Real-World Applications*
- Discuss how fast-germinating seeds might be beneficial in a drought.

# Seed Sprouts

🐛 Predict how long before each type of seed sprouts.

_____     _____

_____     _____

🐛 Make a diagram of your sponge by drawing and labeling the seeds you placed on each section of the sponge.

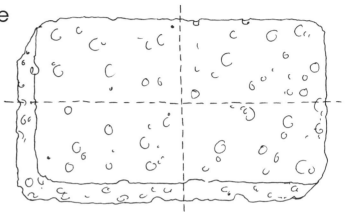

🐛 On what date did you plant your sponge garden?

_____

🐛 Which seed sprouted first? _____

🐛 How many days did it take to sprout? _____

| Grass seed | Lima bean | Mustard seed | Radish seed |
|---|---|---|---|
| Date planted: <br><br> _____ <br><br> #of days to germinate: <br><br> _____ <br><br> Illustrate the roots here: | Date planted: <br><br> _____ <br><br> # of days to germinate: <br><br> _____ <br><br> Illustrate the roots here: | Date planted: <br><br> _____ <br><br> # of days to germinate: <br><br> _____ <br><br> Illustrate the roots here: | Date planted: <br><br> _____ <br><br> # of days to germinate: <br><br> _____ <br><br> Illustrate the roots here: |

# Herbicides and Pesticides

## Gearing Up

Ask the students to name some pests that can destroy our plants. What are some things that can be done to plants to keep pests away? Discuss the negative effects of pesticides.

*Process Skills Used*
- predicting
- role playing

## Guided Discovery

**Background information for the teacher:**
Some insects can be pests to plants. One way to guard against these insects is to spray pesticides on plants. Although these chemicals keep the pests away, they can also harm other animals that might eat the pests or the plants. The harmful effects of pesticides can be seen in this simple food-chain game.

**Materials needed for each small group:**
activity sheet cut into game pieces
two sheets of red and black paper cut into 1-inch (2½ cm) squares
one plastic baggie per grasshopper

**Directions for the activity:**
Explain the concept of a food chain to students. Give each student an animal card and tell the students not to show anyone what they are. Arrange students in a circle and scatter the colored paper on the floor. Tell students that this paper represents plants. First, tell the grasshoppers to eat the plants. They should collect the food by picking up the pieces of paper and placing them in their bags. The grasshoppers remain in the center of the circle. Next, instruct the rodents to eat the grasshoppers. They will eat by tapping a grasshopper on the shoulder. A tapped grasshopper must hand its bag with colored paper to the rodent. Any grasshoppers who have been "eaten" should return to form the circle. Finally, the hawks have 15 seconds to eat. They can tap either rodents or grasshoppers that are remaining. Each one that is tapped must hand the hawk its bag. Then, ask the living grasshoppers or rodents to look in the bags. Tell anyone with black pieces in their bag that they have been poisoned as the black pieces represent pesticides. Now, have the hawks investigate their bags. Although the hawks themselves will not die, their eggs will be very brittle and will not hatch. Students should come to see that there are no winners in this game.

## Responding to Discovery

Discuss why there are no winners in this game.

## Applications and Extensions

Explore other food chains.

*Real-World Applications*
- Discuss the process of growing organic fruits and vegetables.

# Herbicides and Pesticides

| grasshopper | grasshopper | rodent |
|:---:|:---:|:---:|
| grasshopper | grasshopper | rodent |
| grasshopper | grasshopper | rodent |
| grasshopper | grasshopper | rodent |
| grasshopper | grasshopper | rodent |
| grasshopper | grasshopper | rodent |
| grasshopper | grasshopper | rodent |
| grasshopper | grasshopper | rodent |
| grasshopper | grasshopper | rodent |
| grasshopper | grasshopper | rodent |

🐝 If extra roles are needed, add rodents and grasshoppers at a ratio of one rodent for every two grasshoppers.

IF20849 *Flowering Plants*

# Onion-Skin Cells

## Gearing Up

Share *Look Book* by Tana Hoban with the students. The book shows isolated areas of familiar objects. Have the students guess what the object is. If the book is not available, make a small window in a large piece of tagboard. Place the window over a picture of a familiar object. Have the students guess what the whole picture is.

### Process Skills Used
- observing
- recording data
- comparing

## Guided Discovery

**Background information for the teacher:**
All living things are made up of cells. Cells are alive. Cells are the building blocks that make up different living things. Each cell has a unique job.

**Materials needed for each group:**
a microscope, slide, and cover slip
piece of onion skin
iodine

**Directions for the activity:**
Depending on the maturity of your class, you may choose to make the wet-mount slide for the students. To make an onion-cell slide, place a small piece of onion skin on the slide. Put a drop of iodine on top of the specimen. Touch one edge of the droplet with the coverslip and carefully drop it on the side. Blot any leaks and place the slide on the stage of the microscope.

## Responding to Discovery

Students should observe the onion skin and draw the cells. Compare the onion skin cells to the pictures of different cells found in the encyclopedia.

## Applications and Extensions:

Follow this procedure to make cheek-cell slides and have students compare cheek cells to onion-skin cells.

- Use a cotton swab to gently scrape the inside of your cheek. Rub the swab onto a clean slide. Put a drop of iodine on top of the specimen. Touch one edge of the droplet with the coverslip and carefully drop it on the slide. Blot any leaks and place the slide on the stage of the microscope.

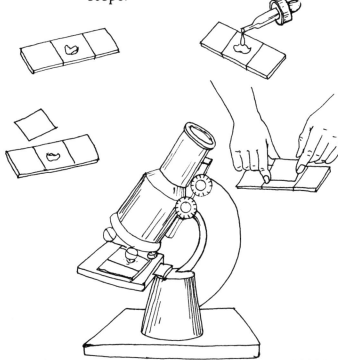

### Real-World Applications
- Discuss how doctors look at human cells to diagnose whether someone is healthy or sick.

# Onion-Skin Cells

| Draw a picture of an onion. | Draw the onion cells. |
|---|---|
| | |

✿ Name other lliving things that have cells.

_____

_____

_____

_____

RED BLOOD CELL

NERVE CELL

MUSCLE CELLS

LEAF PORE GUARD CELL

# Dissecting a Flower

## Gearing Up

Ask students to think about the last time they saw a flower. Did they see any bees or insects around it? Ask them to hypothesize a reason why bees might be seen around flowers. Although many people think of bees as pests, we wouldn't have beautiful flowers without them. Bees help to pollinate flowers and assist them in reproduction of new flowers.

*Process Skills Used*
- observing
- communicating

## Guided Discovery

**Background information for the teacher:**
The main function of a flower is to reproduce and make seeds for future plants. Flowers have an anatomy for that specific purpose. Flowers need other flowers to make seeds. The pollen from the stamen of one flower may travel through the air and settle on the pistil of another. That flower makes seeds in its ovary. Pollen also travels with the help of bees. The pollen from one flower sticks to the legs and bodies of bees. The bees then carry the pollen to other flowers.

**Materials needed for each group:**
a sheet of newspaper
hand lens
a large flower such as a lily or hibiscus

**Directions for the activity:**
Spread the newspaper out on the table and lay the flower on it. Instruct students to examine the flower and write down words to describe its color, size, shape, and other features.

Guide the students as they dissect and draw the parts of their flowers. Count the petals. Remove the stamen. The stamen makes pollen, which the flower must share with another flower to make seeds. Look for pollen. Remove the pistil and gently rub the stamen on the pistil. What do you observe? Use your fingernail to gently slit and open the ovary. Sometimes the ovary is called the seedpod.

## Responding to Discovery

- What is the advantage of a flower having colorful petals? (it attracts insects.)
- What are two ways that pollen travels from flower to flower?
- What did you see inside the ovary?

## Applications and Extensions:

Dissect a different type of flower and compare the parts. A geranium works well.

*Real-World Applications*
- Compare plant reproduction to that of humans and animals.

Name _____

# Dissecting a Flower

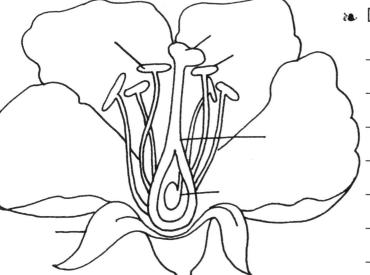

🌱 Describe your flower.

_____
_____
_____
_____
_____
_____
_____

🌱 After taking apart the flower, draw each of the sections below. Use your hand lens to observe the details. Below each illustration, tell the function of each flower part.

| Petals | Stamen | Pistil | Ovary |
|---|---|---|---|
| | | | |
| Function: | Function: | Function: | Function: |

🌱 What are ways in which pollination takes place?

1. _____

2. _____

          IF20849 *Flowering Plants*

# Life Cycle of a Flowering Plant

## Gearing Up

Gather six boys and six girls. Have them line up in an alternating pattern. Ask the students to identify the pattern and ask who could be next to continue the pattern. Then have the line move into a circle. Note how the pattern continues indefinitely. This is a cycle—a pattern that repeats in a circle.

> ### Process Skills Used
> • making a model

## Guided Discovery

**Background information for the teacher:**
The pollinated flower wilts away and the ovary changes into fruit. Seeds form inside the fruit.

**Materials needed for each group:**
construction paper
glue
crayons
seeds
plastic flowers with leaves

**Directions for the activity:**
Have each student draw the life cycle of the flowering plant. The steps include the following:

1. seed
2. seedling
3. adult plant
4. adult plant with flowers
5. adult plant with fruit. (back to step 1)

The students may glue actual seeds and (plastic) flowers onto their cycles for a 3-D effect.

## Responding to Discovery

Using their models, students should describe the stages of the life cycle.

## Applications and Extensions

Brainstorm a list of fruits and flowering plants. Discuss natural ways that the seeds could get replanted to continue the cycle. Discuss ways in which humans change the cycle.

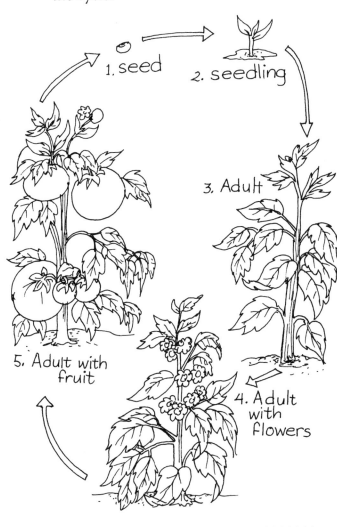

1. seed
2. seedling
3. Adult
4. Adult with flowers
5. Adult with fruit

> ### Real-World Applications
> • Discuss other life cycles.

IF20849 *Flowering Plants*

# Life Cycle of a Flowering Plant

Label the stages of the cycle.

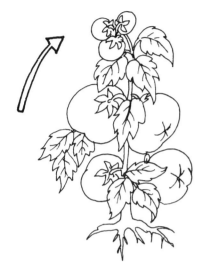

1. _____

5. _____

**The Life Cycle of a Flowering Plant**

2. _____

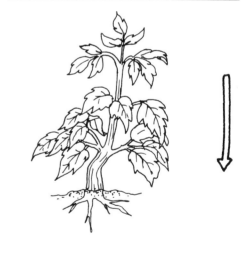

3. _____

4. _____

IF20849 *Flowering Plants*

# Investigating a Pumpkin

## Gearing Up

Ask students to guess what you are describing.

"I grow in a patch on a vine. I am a member of the gourd family. I am orange and contain many seeds. My meat is used to make pie, and my seeds are quite tasty."

> ### Process Skills Used
> - observing
> - predicting
> - inferring
> - measuring
> - recording data

## Guided Discovery

**Background information for the teacher:**
This activity contains many parts, and you may want to do it over a period of several days. Save the activities that involve cutting open the pumpkin until last.

**Materials needed for the whole class:**
one large pumpkin
a small empty wastebasket
water and paper towels
spoons
tape measure
a scale
a dishpan
a sharp knife

**Directions for the activity:**
**Activity 1:** Place an empty wastebasket in a dishpan and fill the wastebasket to the rim with water. Place the pumpkin in the water and allow the excess water that is displaced to spill over into the dishpan. To find the volume of the pumpkin, measure the water that was displaced. Did the pumpkin sink or float?

**Activity 2:** Allow students to take turns weighing the pumpkin on a scale. Use a tape measure to measure the diameter of the pumpkin.

**Activity 3:** Cut the pumpkin into pieces and have students measure the thickness of the meaty part of the pumpkin. Ask students to predict how many seeds are in the pumpkin. Then give each student a handful of seeds so they can count the seeds collectively. Measure the mass of one seed using a balance scale. Ask students to infer the mass of all the seeds.

## Responding to Discovery

Complete the student activity sheet. Have students describe the pumpkin using all the senses.

## Applications and Extensions

Make pumpkin pie or roasted pumpkin seeds.

> ### Real-World Applications
> - Brainstorm the many uses of the pumpkin.

Name _____

# Investigating a Pumpkin

Observe the pumpkin and answer the following questions.

- What is the volume of the pumpkin? (How much water was displaced?) _____

- Does the pumpkin sink or float? _____

- How much does the pumpkin weigh? _____

- What is the diameter? _____

- How many seeds do you predict are in the pumpkin? _____

- How many seeds are in your handful? _____

- How many seeds are in the whole pumpkin? _____

- How much does one seed weigh? _____

- How much do you think all of the seeds weigh? _____

- How thick is the meaty section? _____

- List as many uses as you can think of for a pumpkin.

_____

_____

_____

_____

_____

_____

_____

_____

IF20849 *Flowering Plants*

# Erosion and Plants

## Gearing Up

Ask the students if they have ever built a sand castle on the beach. Do they think that the sand castle is still standing? The students will probably know that the water has since washed it away. Maybe they saw the water wash it away. Tell them that the action of the water on the sand is similar to the way erosion works on the land.

*Process Skills Used*
- making a model
- predicting
- observing
- recording data

## Guided Discovery

**Background information for the teacher:**
Erosion occurs when rocks and soil are moved from one place to another. Weathering by wind or rain causes erosion. Plants play an important part in helping to slow down or prevent some types of erosion. When the roots of a plant anchor themselves into the soil, it helps to hold the soil together.

**Materials needed:**
aluminum baking pan
identical pan containing sod (soil and grass)
soil
metric ruler
a paper cup
marker
6 toothpicks
water
bucket
2-inch (5 cm) wood block

**Directions for the activity:**
Fill the first aluminum pan 2 cm high with packed soil. Use a pencil point to poke small holes in the bottom of the paper cup so that you can use it to sprinkle water over the pan and simulate rain. Mark a line at the 2 cm mark of the six toothpicks. Push them into the soil in three rows with two toothpicks in each row. Tilt the pan and place the wood block underneath it to act as a wedge.

Sprinkle 2 cups of water over the soil. Use the bucket to catch the runoff. Repeat the process with the pan containing the sod. Students will find that the pan with the grass barely eroded. The grass held the soil together.

## Responding to Discovery

Discuss the following questions: Which soil eroded the most? Which soil eroded the least? Why do you think these results occurred? How are plants important in helping to stop or slow down erosion? Where could plants help control erosion?

## Applications and Extensions

Simulate erosion on a potted plant with a more sophisticated root system.

*Real-World Applications*
- Plants such as sea grasses are planted along the banks of beaches. This helps to keep the sand from washing away.

© Instructional Fair • TS Denison

IF20849 *Flowering Plants*

# Erosion and Plants

🌱 What do you think will happen when you sprinkle water over the soil?

_____

_____

_____

_____

Draw the pan of soil before and after you add the water.

| | |
|---|---|
| | |
| before | after |

🌱 What do you think will happen when you sprinkle water over the grassy soil?

_____

_____

_____

_____

Draw the grassy soil before and after you add the water.

| | |
|---|---|
| | |
| before | after |

🌱 Which soil eroded the most? _____

🌱 Why do you think the grass changed the erosion?

_____

🌱 What is erosion, and how does it affect our earth?

_____

_____

🌱 Where do you think erosion is a problem? Why?

_____

_____

# Performance-Based Assessment

3 = Exceeds expectations
2 = Consistently meets expectations
1 = Below expectations

**Student Names**

## Lesson Investigation Discovery

| | | | | | | | | | | | |
|---|---|---|---|---|---|---|---|---|---|---|---|
| Lesson 1:  Seed Sort | | | | | | | | | | | |
| Lesson 2:  Fruity Tooty | | | | | | | | | | | |
| Lesson 3:  Do Plants Need Light? | | | | | | | | | | | |
| Lesson 4:  Do Plants Need Water? | | | | | | | | | | | |
| Lesson 5:  Soil Soak | | | | | | | | | | | |
| Lesson 6:  Super Stem! | | | | | | | | | | | |
| Lesson 7:  Found a Peanut | | | | | | | | | | | |
| Lesson 8:  Seed Sprouts | | | | | | | | | | | |
| Lesson 9:  Herbicides and Pesticides | | | | | | | | | | | |
| Lesson 10:  Onion-Skin Cells | | | | | | | | | | | |
| Lesson 11:  Dissecting a Flower | | | | | | | | | | | |
| Lesson 12:  Life Cycle of a Flowering Plant | | | | | | | | | | | |
| Lesson 13:  Investigating a Pumpkin | | | | | | | | | | | |
| Lesson 14:  Erosion and Plants | | | | | | | | | | | |

## Specific Lesson Skills

| | | | | | | | | | | | |
|---|---|---|---|---|---|---|---|---|---|---|---|
| Can make reasonable predictions. | | | | | | | | | | | |
| Can make detailed observations. | | | | | | | | | | | |
| Can propose an explanation. | | | | | | | | | | | |
| Can follow written directions. | | | | | | | | | | | |
| Can use a ruler and measure to the nearest centimeter. | | | | | | | | | | | |
| Can work cooperatively with a partner or group. | | | | | | | | | | | |
| Can build on observations by asking appropriate questions. | | | | | | | | | | | |
| Can create a graph based on data from investigations. | | | | | | | | | | | |
| Can use a magnifying glass. | | | | | | | | | | | |
| Participates in discussions. | | | | | | | | | | | |
| Can find mass to nearest gram. | | | | | | | | | | | |
| Can communicate through writing, drawing, and dialogue. | | | | | | | | | | | |
| Can apply what is learned to real-world situations. | | | | | | | | | | | |

IF20849 *Flowering Plants*